Margaret Mead

Margaret Mead

The World Was Her Family

SUSAN SAUNDERS

illustrated by Ted Lewin

PUFFIN BOOKS

PUFFIN BOOKS
An imprint of Penguin Random House LLC
375 Hudson Street
New York, New York 10014

First published in the United States of America by Viking Penguin Inc., 1987
Published by Puffin Books, 1988
Reissued by Puffin Books, an imprint of Penguin Random House LLC, 2015

LIBRARY OF CONGRESS CATALOGING-IN-PUBLICATION DATA
Saunders, Susan.
Margaret Mead: the world was her family.
(Women of our time)
Summary: Examines the life of the pioneer anthropologist who popularized the
field and used her ideas to promote world unity and peace.
ISBN 978-0-670-81051-2 (hardcover)
1. Mead, Margaret, 1901–1978—Juvenile literature.
2. Anthropologists—United States—Biography—Juvenile Literature.
{1. Mead, Margaret, 1901–1978. 2. Anthropologists}
I. Lewin, Ted ill. II. Title. III. Series.
GN21.M36 S28 1987

Puffin Books ISBN 978-0-14-751661-9

Printed in the United States of America

1 3 5 7 9 10 8 6 4 2

To Beth Greenfeld,
for her interest and assistance

CONTENTS

one

"THERE'S NO ONE LIKE MARGARET"

Margaret Mead lived in sixty different houses before she was a teenager. Moving so often taught her to make the best of new situations. It also made people, not places or things, most important to her. In each new place, Margaret carefully watched the people around her to decide how she would fit in, how her life would mesh with theirs.

Studying people—figuring out the parts they played in their families and in the world outside—was to become Margaret's life's work.

She began by studying her own family. At a very early age, she said, she compared her family with other families, those she knew or had heard about. Margaret wondered why they were different, and why they were alike. . . .

Margaret's father was the reason for all the moving in her childhood. Edward Sherwood Mead was a professor of economics at the University of Pennsylvania (economics describes how money works in the world). As a part of his job, he helped set up branches of the university across the state. His family sometimes went with him and sometimes stayed behind in houses they rented in and around Philadelphia.

Margaret's mother, Emily Fogg Mead, was a teacher and sociologist. Sociologists are concerned with conditions of society, such as crime and poverty, and its institutions, such as marriage, the family, and school. She postponed her career to raise her children, but she never stopped studying. For Emily, Margaret would say later, work was everything.

Margaret was born in Philadelphia on December 16, 1901. The Meads' first baby, she was loved and wanted. Margaret's mother filled thirteen notebooks with details about her behavior as an infant and a toddler.

Golden haired and blue-eyed, Margaret was a sturdy, willful little girl. She always had to know everything that was going on in the household. If she felt she had been left out of anything interesting, she was given to short but noisy fits of anger—Margaret was an enthusiastic door-slammer. Her father's pet name for her was Punk.

Over and over again, she heard, "There's no one like Margaret." Margaret was eveyone's favorite, especially her grandmother's. Martha Ramsey Mead had been a schoolteacher in Ohio. She came to live with her son and his wife soon after they were married. Grandma Mead was to give Margaret many things: love, affection, and a model of her own firmness and strength of character. Margaret found it comforting that she knew exactly where she stood with her grandmother. "Grandma meant what she said, always," Margaret remembered.

As she cooked, or embroidered, or worked in the garden, Grandma Mead would tell Margaret stories of her own girlhood back in Ohio. Those early days became as real to Margaret as if she had lived them herself. The Ohio tales presented her with still another family to think about.

When Margaret was two and a half, her only brother, Richard, was born. Emily Mead would devote four notebooks to her son.

Margaret is supposed to have complained when Richard was a toddler, "Can't you say anything but 'da da da' all the time?" She had wanted a brother she could get into mischief with, but Richard was frail. Often kept indoors with colds or earaches, Richard was a disappointment as a playmate.

It was to the third child that Margaret gave

her wholehearted attention. She was four when the baby was born, and was allowed to name her herself.

Katherine was a lively, happy infant, and Margaret delighted in caring for her. One day, Margaret decided she could manage the younger children very well without any adult help. Leading Richard by the hand and carrying Katherine, she went off to the nursery and locked the door. Getting food wouldn't be difficult. Margaret planned to sneak out in the middle of the night for it, while the grown-ups slept.

Her mother pleaded with her through the door for an hour. Margaret finally gave in, but only because she couldn't solve the problem of the bathroom—it was in a different part of the house.

There was one wonderful Christmas with Katherine, with a huge tree, and a doll dressed in white fur. Then, in March, Katherine died. She was nine months old.

After Katherine's death, Edward Mead said

he would never give so much love to a child again. In his sorrow, he blamed his grieving wife for not having called the doctor sooner.

Richard was too young to understand what had happened to Katherine. He wandered forlornly through the house calling her name for months afterward. "I knew she had died," Margaret wrote later, "but my little lost sister lived on in my daydreams. At first I dreamed about a lost twin sister. Then I dreamed of finding Katherine herself again."

When a second little sister, Elizabeth, was born two years later, Margaret said it gave her the faith to believe that "what was lost would always be found." Seven years younger than Margaret, Elizabeth became her delight. The last member of the family, Priscilla, arrived eighteen months after Elizabeth.

Grandma Mead encouraged Margaret to take notes on the little girls. In a notebook, Margaret recorded their first words, how they imitated each other, how they were different.

Margaret
and Emily Mead
1905

Neither Edward nor Emily Mead had recovered enough from the death of Katherine to give the new babies much attention. In many ways, Margaret thought of her sisters as her own children, both to study and to teach.

She wanted them to have things she felt she had missed as a child—a little gold locket, hats with long ribbons, lacy petticoats instead of the more sensible bloomers she had worn. When the girls were older, she gave them both lockets as presents. Then she found out Elizabeth and Priscilla had never wanted lockets. Not only were her sisters very different from each other, they were different from Margaret. Again she wondered what made the differences.

two

DON'T SIT STILL FOR MORE THAN AN HOUR

Until she was eleven, most of Margaret's schooling took place at home. Together, Grandma Mead and Margaret's mother taught Margaret and her brother and sisters.

Grandma Mead had a rule: children shouldn't have to sit still for more than an hour at a time. "Grandma—and Mother— were more interested in the freedom to move," Margaret said. Her grandmother also believed that arithmetic was harmful to young minds, so Margaret learned her multiplication tables, then went directly into algebra, skipping the rest of arithmetic altogether.

Margaret would not be well versed in spelling or geography. Her grandmother was against drills and memorizing long lists of facts. Instead, a lesson might start with a description of a plant. Then Margaret would be sent outdoors to find examples. She learned to look carefully at the world, and to remember exactly what she had seen.

Margaret did as much reading as she could—for her birthday she was usually given one serious book and one silly one. However, too much reading was thought to be bad for a child. It became one of Margaret's secret pleasures to read at night when she should have been sleeping, or "in the daytime hours . . . curled up in a hollow in the roots of a tree."

Emily, Margaret's mother, felt that children's hands should be trained as well as their minds. Each time the family moved, she sought out craftsmen in the area. The Mead children learned carpentry, basketmaking, carving, and weaving.

The Meads moved to a farm in the Buckingham Valley of Pennsylvania when Margaret was eleven: "Grandma believed every child had a right to grow up on a farm." There was a brook running through the property, a bridge and a ravine and an orchard. A huge three-story barn proved to be perfect for games of hide-and-seek.

In the past year, Margaret had gained forty pounds and grown from the size of a seven-year-old to her adult height of a little over five feet one inch.

Along with another former "city" child, Margaret organized a club of about fifteen children called the Buckingham Climbers Club. They climbed trees and fences, staged plays in the Meads' barn, and had baseball games. Margaret was never very good at sports, but she insisted on setting up the rules and managing the teams.

SUSAN SAUNDERS

The children raced around the countryside in a horse and buggy and on a friend's pony. Still, there was never enough going on to suit Margaret. She longed for even more people, for more exciting things to do.

Margaret jumped at the chance to go to school, first a private school in the village of Buckingham, then a public high school in the larger town of Doylestown. School, she soon discovered, was a system she could learn, as she had learned to settle into new houses in new towns. In fact, Margaret learned it almost too easily. "No one had to study very hard, and if there was good ice . . . we all went ice skating." None of the teachers inspired her as much as her grandmother had.

To keep from being bored, Margaret wrote. She began a novel. She wrote short plays, which were performed by the drama club. She started a school magazine. She also began to think about having a career. She imagined herself a writer, a lawyer, a minister's wife with six children.

When the Mead family moved to the farm, Margaret had joined a church. Neither of her parents was religious, and Grandma Mead had stopped going to the Methodist church when Margaret was an infant.

Margaret, however, was allowed to attend many different church services with friends and neighbors. A nearness to God, Margaret thought, came from feelings, not beliefs. The service at the Episcopal church in Buckingham put into words her own feelings about God. Choosing her godparents herself—Isobel Lord, an old friend of Margaret's mother, and Miss Lucia, daughter of the rector of the Episcopal church—Margaret was baptized.

No one in her family really understood why she wanted to be baptized. Margaret's father teased her about it. The other children Margaret knew went to church only because they had to. But as she put it, "I needed an anchorage," something she could always depend on. Margaret liked praying. She liked church. She grew very close to Miss Lucia, who was to be a friend until the older woman's death.

Miss Lucia was the kind of person Margaret wanted to be: selfless, kind, and, like Grandma Mead, firm and loving. It was the shining example set by her godmother that made the life of a minister's wife attractive to Margaret.

It also added to Luther Cressman's appeal. Luther was the brother of George Cressman, a science teacher at Margaret's high school. George had been invited to the Meads' farm for dinner one June evening in 1917. He brought along his younger brother, who was visiting.

Luther was slender, redheaded, and blue-eyed. He could drive a car and shoot a gun—the six Cressman boys had been raised on a farm. Luther was a senior at Pennsylvania State College, where he studied Latin and Greek. And he was thinking of becoming a clergyman.

That night, Luther and Margaret "danced and danced" at the prom at the high school. The very successful evening was followed only a few hours later for Margaret by an attack of appendicitis. She spent several months recovering from the operation she had to have, so she didn't see Luther again that summer. They wrote to each other—Luther sent her some books of poetry and his yearbook.

The following Christmas vacation, Margaret visited Luther's family. There was ice-skating, and the couple took long walks in the snow. It was on one of these walks under the bright winter stars that Luther told Margaret he loved her. "I love you, too," Margaret answered. They kissed, and, barely sixteen, Margaret became engaged to be married.

That spring, Luther graduated from college—Margaret missed his graduation because she had German measles—and Margaret from high school. They kept their engagement a secret through the next year. "I

Luther Cressman

wrote Luther every day," Margaret said. "Four pages in small, fine handwriting." Margaret spent the year at a new school, cramming three years of French into two semesters, as well as studying trigonometry.

She needed the courses to enter Welles-ley College in Massachusetts in the fall of 1919. Wellesley had been Margaret's mother's college—she was forced to drop out when her own father's business failed. Margaret was to have the same kind of disappointment. Edward Mead, too, had lost money. He informed Margaret that he couldn't afford to send her to Wellesley.

He had recently been told that Luther and Margaret were engaged. Why, Margaret's father asked, did she need college at all, since she was planning to get married?

Margaret was angry and upset. She felt strongly that college was the gateway to the rest of life. It was "as necessary as learning to read." After many arguments, Margaret's mother talked her husband into changing his mind. Margaret would not go East to Wellesley, however. She would travel West to Edward Mead's own college: DePauw, in the small town of Greencastle, Indiana.

three

Margaret was eagerly looking forward to college. She had packed her books and pictures, and she had chosen her clothes carefully. She especially liked an evening dress she had designed—made by a dressmaker—in colors of red, green, blue, and white. To Margaret, it called to mind red poppies blooming in a field of green wheat, with a blue sky and white clouds.

In DePauw, she wore it confidently to a party at a sorority, one of many girls' clubs on campus. She soon found out the dress was wrong, her eastern accent was wrong—*she* was wrong.

As Margaret said later, the word went around that inviting her to the party had been a mistake. She would not get a bid to join that sorority, or any of the others at DePauw. Since all parties and most campus events centered on the girls' and boys' clubs, Margaret would have no social life at all.

The freshmen who were joining sororities wouldn't talk to Margaret. Those who had not been invited to join wouldn't, either— they didn't want to call attention to their own unpopularity. For the first time, Margaret was left out of activities. She said it was the only time she would experience real discrimination—unfair treatment because she was different. It opened her eyes to the many wrongs in the world. It also hurt.

Margaret set out to show what she could do. She wrote a skit to be performed by her dormitory. She wrote and directed the college May celebration and designed the freshman float. She succeeded in getting an older friend, Katherine Rothenberger, elected vice president of her class.

Not only did Margaret have brains, Katherine said, but she knew how to use them. The sororities would come to recognize that Margaret was not somebody they could ignore.

Margaret thought some of her teachers were excellent, but coeducation—boys and girls in the same class—was a problem for her. In the Mead family, it was believed that bright girls could—and *should*—do better than bright boys. Margaret's father had always insisted that her grades be at least two and a half points higher than her brother's.

At DePauw, Margaret discovered, girls who did better in class than boys would suffer for it socially. It seemed to Margaret that it would make more sense to go to a girls' school, if she wanted to do her best.

At the end of her freshman year, Margaret's father agreed to allow her to transfer to another college. She chose Barnard in New York City, a women's college that was part of Columbia University. After a year in Indiana, Margaret felt that New York was the "center of life," and she couldn't wait to get there. Luther Cressman was in New York already, studying to be an Episcopal minister at the General Theological Seminary.

At Barnard College in 1920, Margaret Mead found the "kind of student life that matched [her] earlier dreams." She made friends who would last her lifetime.

There was only one dormitory at Barnard then. The overflow of students lived in groups in apartments near the campus. Most of Margaret's group of six or so girls remained together from year to year and from apartment to apartment. Each year they adopted for their nickname something critical that had been said about them, or about Barnard students in general—"Mental and Moral Muss" was one, "Communist Morons" another. The name that stuck, however, was the "Ash Can Cats."

In the Ash Can Cats, Margaret found young women who were quick, intelligent, energetic, amusing, who loved to talk and to argue as much as she did. Of Margaret and the others, Luther Cressman said, "The rate at which things are going on in your heads all the time! It just tires me to think about it!"

Margaret and Luther arranged blind dates for college dances between Margaret's friends at Barnard and Luther's at the seminary. Margaret always wore a black dress to the dances, and her glasses. As she explained, "I didn't take my glasses off to look prettier, because it was more important to see people on the other side of the dance floor, keep an eye on people I had brought to the dance." She wasn't going to be left out of anything ever again.

Margaret and Luther saw each other one or two times a week, going for walks, or to plays and concerts. Their engagement was comfortable, but not very demanding. Margaret didn't have to worry about getting dates, or about not having a boyfriend. Being engaged to Luther, she said, gave her the time to devote to her friendships with women.

"We learned loyalty to women," Margaret wrote much later of her college friends, "pleasure in conversation with women, and . . . delight in one another's minds."

One of her closest friends—and the most talented member of the Ash Can Cats—was the poet Léonie Adams. Knowing Léonie helped Margaret realize that, while she wrote well, she would not have a career as a creative writer. At DePauw, Margaret had been an English major. At Barnard, she began to study psychology, the science of the mind.

A career in science would allow, Margaret felt, for different levels and different kinds of talent. In science, her work would count. Margaret had chosen one of the social sciences—the others were economics, sociology, and history—because she was interested in people.

As she continued to study, she wavered between psychology and sociology, her mother's field. Not until Margaret was a senior did she take the class that would set the course for her life.

At that time, a fellow student said, Margaret was like "a missile waiting to be directed." She would find her direction in an anthropology class.

Anthropology is the study of mankind: its beginnings, its development, its beliefs and customs. Margaret had been studying people since she was a child—her family, her friends, and their families—sorting out their similarities and differences. And anthropology is based on such comparisons.

The class Margaret took was taught by

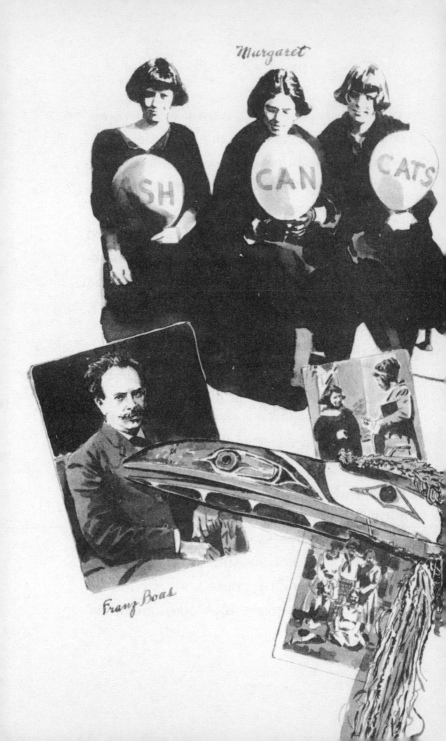

Margaret

SH CAN CATS

Franz Boas

Professor Franz Boas. Professor Boas was one of the most outspoken anthropologists of his time, and the best known. Born in Germany, he had lived with Eskimos in the Arctic and Native Americans in the Pacific Northwest.

All people are faced with the same basic problems, Boas said: how to find food and shelter, how to organize their families, how to rear children. By studying other groups of people, one might learn better ways of solving these problems and, at the same time, understand one's own life better.

Anthropology offered a way of studying primitive peoples—those without a written history or a knowledge of modern science. More anthropologists were needed, fast, to record the lives of these people before their old ways were swept up by the twentieth century.

"Franz Boas was the greatest mind I had ever encountered," Margaret said. She found Boas's class so exciting that she decided to sign up for every course he taught. She became friendly with Ruth Benedict, the professor's assistant. By the spring of her senior year, with Ruth's encouragement, Margaret had chosen anthropology as her career.

four

A PEOPLE OF HER OWN

That June, in 1923, Margaret graduated from Barnard with honors. The following September, she and Luther were married at the little Episcopal church in Buckingham. With Luther's agreement, Margaret Mead had decided to keep her own name. To her outraged father she explained, "I'm going to be famous some day, and I'm going to be known by my own name."

The couple moved into a two-room apartment in New York City. Luther was acting as a part-time pastor in a Brooklyn parish while he continued his studies. Margaret worked for an economics professor and took graduate courses in anthropology at Columbia University.

To get a graduate degree in anthropology, Margaret would have to do fieldwork, to study a particular group of people firsthand, recording exactly how they lived. Franz Boas wanted Margaret to remain in the United States, where she would study Native Americans.

So many anthropologists had studied them already that Native Americans were becoming resentful about it. There was a joke at the time about the usual Native American family. It had four members, the joke went: a mother, a father, a baby . . . and an anthropologist. Margaret wanted a new "people," a people of her own.

The people she had in mind lived on a remote string of islands called Tuamotu (say "Too-ah-MO-too"). Tuamotu was on the other side of the world in the South Pacific. Too far away, Boas said, and too dangerous. What if Margaret became seriously ill? She might even be killed—anthropologists had been.

Margaret complained to her father that Boas was insisting she study Native Americans, while she wanted to go someplace much more interesting. Perhaps Edward Mead didn't like the idea of anyone else telling his daughter what to do. He took her side. He would give her the money for a trip around the world.

Boas finally agreed. Margaret could go to the South Pacific—but she must choose an island that a boat visited regularly. Margaret had wanted to study change in the lives of the people; Boas insisted that she study adolescent girls—teenagers—instead. There was a question he wanted answered: do teenagers the world over have the same problems? Or do they behave differently in different societies?

Anthropologists at that time had a very basic disagreement. Some thought that human behavior was inherited, that people were born with many important differences that wouldn't change as they grew older. Some anthropologists—Franz Boas was one of them—believed that differences in behavior were learned in the world outside. Margaret, Boas hoped, would be able to prove he was correct.

Up to now, anthropologists had paid very little attention to women. Boaz thought Margaret would be right for studying young women. Margaret said later that maybe he chose her because of her appearance. She was twenty-three years old. But with her quick step and light voice, weighing under one hundred pounds, and not much more than five feet tall, Margaret seemed like a teenager herself.

At last it was decided. Margaret would travel to American Samoa, where she would study teenage girls.

Luther Cressman would be in France for the year that Margaret was gone. Their life together—which was to be centered on the church—was slowly coming apart. Luther had begun to teach sociology courses. Margaret became more and more involved with her work and with fellow anthropologists. As his wife boarded the train at the beginning of her journey, Luther realized that the future of their marriage was very uncertain.

Margaret traveled by train to California, then by steamer to Hawaii. She had never been to sea before. She stayed in Honolulu for two weeks with a Wellesley friend of her mother's. Margaret studied objects from the South Pacific at a local museum. A botanist showed her the plants she would find in Samoa. She was introduced to two half-Samoan children whose family would be able to help her when she arrived there.

Margaret had an uncomfortable cruise on a small ship that rolled across the swells of the Pacific. She at last reached Pago Pago (say "Pango-Pango"), on the island of Tutuila ("Too-too-EE-la") in American Samoa. It was

August 31, 1925. The American fleet was docked in the harbor. Bands were playing, and there were even airplanes overhead. Most of the Samoans Margaret saw were dressed as she was, instead of in the flowered wraparound skirts called lavalavas. They were selling gift items to American sailors. Tutuila was not the quiet tropical island Margaret had imagined.

She didn't give herself time to feel disappointed. She moved into an old hotel and set right to work. First she had to learn the language. For one hour a day, Margaret took lessons from a young Samoan nurse, G. F. Pepe. Pepe would pronouce a word: "*Talofa*" ("Tah-LOW-fah"). Then she would tell Margaret what it meant: "Love to you," which the Samoans said instead of "Good morning" or "Good evening." Then Margaret would write the word down as it sounded to her. For seven more hours, Margaret would study the words Pepe had taught her, and memorize more words from a Samoan-English dictionary put together by Christian missionaries.

Samoan was difficult for Margaret. At the end of six weeks, however, she felt she knew it well enough to manage without an interpreter. She traveled to a nearby village. The mother of the two children Margaret had met in Hawaii had arranged for her to stay in the village chief's house.

Margaret had told no one she was married—she wanted to appear to be as much like the teenage girls she would study as possible. Unmarried women in Samoa could not have their own houses. Margaret was made an honorary member of the chief's family and given the name of Makelita ("Mah-keh-LEE-tah").

The chief's nineteen-year-old daughter, Fa'amotu ("Fah-ah-MO-too"), taught Margaret some of the rules of Samoan behavior: how to sit cross-legged and straight-backed on mats on the pebbled floor; how to eat properly with her fingers; how to serve kava, a ceremonial drink; the words to use when she talked to chiefs; how to dance.

The children of the village avoided her, however. As a member of the chief's family, Margaret was too grand for them to speak to.

In Pago Pago again, Margaret met Ruth Holt, a young woman who lived with her husband, Edward, at a naval medical station on Ta'u ("Tow," rhyming with "now"). Ta'u was an island a hundred miles away from Tutuila. The Holts, their two children, and two sailors were the only white people on the island. They lived within walking distance of three Samoan villages.

Margaret wrote to Franz Boas that Ta'u was more unspoiled than other parts of Samoa. She would be able to live with the Holts, yet be within a few minutes' walk of the teenagers she wanted to study. And she could eat American food. The Samoan diet of yams, bananas, breadfruit, and taro roots was too starchy for her.

Later, anthropologists would criticize Margaret for not living in one of the villages. If she had lived with a Samoan family, Margaret argued, she would have had no privacy. Most Samoan houses were one large room, usually with no walls at all because of the steamy heat. The roof, thatched with sugarcane—protection from the rain that fell four or five times a day—was held up by thick wooden posts. All of the family would have been in the room with Margaret. The room would have been open to the stares and comments of passing villagers as well. How could Margaret have made the children feel comfortable enough to share their secrets with her?

Margaret chose fifty girls to study from a population of about one thousand people spread over three villages. The girls' ages ranged from seven to twenty. Margaret went swimming with them. She went to their church services on Sundays. She watched them take care of their younger brothers and sisters. She

Margaret
and the
chief's
daughter

Breadfruit

went on fishing trips with them and worked beside them in the village gardens. Margaret learned the background of all the girls she was studying. At the same time, she grew to be their friend. Then she listened to them talk.

Boas had told Margaret that she must be prepared to waste a lot of time just sitting still and listening. Sitting still was very hard for someone with Margaret's energy, but she did it. The girls talked about their families and boyfriends and about getting married.

Margaret spent every day listening. In the evening, she joined their dancing. At night, she was busy going over the notes she had taken.

Margaret often worked fifteen hours a day—"as many hours as I could stay awake," she said. Her greatest relief came from reading letters from friends and family—which arrived every three weeks on the government steamship—and answering them. She wanted to let the people back home know exactly what she was doing and learning. The letters forced her to sort out her thoughts, to make things clear for an audience.

Margaret's work was interrupted by a huge tropical storm. Along with the Holt family and the two sailors, she waited it out in a concrete water tank. When they climbed out of the tank at daybreak, the Holts' house was the only wooden structure on the island still standing. Margaret continued her work as the island rebuilt.

In June 1926, Margaret returned to Pago Pago with answers to Boas's question. *Did* teenagers have the same problems in very different parts of the world?

There was little reason for teenage girls to rebel against their parents in Samoa, Margaret found. If there was a disagreement, a girl simply moved to a relative's house. Since girls had no "best" friend, but a large group of friends, there was no jealousy. The same could be said of their boyfriends. Girls rarely saw only one boy at a time. A girl had many boy-friends before her arranged marriage to a young man her parents had picked out.

Nor was there any hurry to get married. For Samoan girls, the period between the time they stopped babysitting for their little brothers and sisters and started caring for their own children was one to be enjoyed for as long as possible. On the other hand, there were no fears about being an adult. All Samoan girls knew how to do the few things they would need to do as married women: prepare food, weave mats, care for children. Samoan adolescents, Margaret concluded, had few of the difficulties usually associated with teenagers.

Years later, critics would say she was wrong, that nothing was so simple. Perhaps Margaret hadn't understood the language well enough, they said—no one could hope to learn Samoan in such a short time. Perhaps the Samoans had told her what they thought she wanted to hear. Perhaps Margaret was too eager to please

Boas, and ignored information that didn't lead to the answer he wanted.

Others would spring to defend Margaret's work. What she had found out in Samoa wasn't wrong, they said. At most, it was incomplete. She was just learning how to do fieldwork. Besides, the Samoa of today was different from Margaret's Samoa of the 1920s.

Luther Cressman was to write, more than fifty years after Margaret's trip, that she had proved what *she* had set out to prove in Samoa: that a woman anthropologist could do fieldwork outside of North America—nine thousand miles outside—as well as any man.

In less than three years, her findings would be published in a book called *Coming of Age in Samoa*. Overnight, Margaret Mead would become the most famous anthropologist in the world.

five

Margaret sailed to Sydney, Australia, to catch a steamship to Europe. She planned to meet Luther and one of her friends from the Ash Can Cats in France, then join Ruth Benedict in Rome. Margaret had just spent nine months with no one to talk to about books, or feelings, or her work. Now she thought she would be facing a six-week voyage more or less alone. On the ship, however, she met a young psychologist from New Zealand, Reo Fortune.

A handsome man with black hair and blue eyes, Reo was on his way to England, to study at Cambridge University. He was as eager for talk as Margaret was.

Like Luther, Reo had studied Greek and Latin in college. Then he had turned to philosophy and psychology. He fascinated Margaret because, growing up in rural New Zealand, he had never seen a play performed, or seen an original painting, or heard a symphony orchestra—but he had read everything he could lay his hands on. He was studying dreams—and Margaret began to dream more than she ever had in her life. Margaret had no liking for games, but Reo played chess, so Margaret played chess. Above all, they talked. Halfway through the voyage, Margaret and Reo realized they were falling in love.

When the boat docked, Luther Cressman was waiting for Margaret. She was the last one off. She had stayed as long as she could with Reo.

Margaret saw Reo twice more that summer, but by the fall, she and Luther were together in New York City. Luther had given up the ministry and was teaching at City College. Margaret began her first job, at the American Museum of Natural History.

Her office was in the top of one of the towers of the big stone building. Margaret would spend her life in rented apartments, or sharing the houses of friends. But the office in the museum tower would remain her permanent home, from the fall of 1926 until her death in 1978. She hung a Samoan woven mat on the wall and settled in.

That winter, Margaret taught a class at Columbia University and worked on her notes about Samoa. She was not aiming her report at other scientists. She wanted everyone to understand—and perhaps use—what she had learned. Margaret was already beginning to do what scientists would criticize her for later: "popularize" anthropology.

A publisher suggested she add more about how the things she had learned in Samoa related to American teenagers. Margaret was more than willing—she had already begun to give talks on just that topic.

Margaret's friends were beginning to worry about her, however. Discouraged about her marriage, Margaret was feeling very blue. In the early summer, she traveled to Europe, where she met Reo again. Finally, from Berlin, she wrote Luther that their life together was over.

That fall, Margaret took an apartment alone in New York. Her work about Samoa was accepted by the publisher. By the following summer, Margaret and Luther were divorced.

Margaret joined Reo Fortune in Australia, where they were married in October 1928. Then they sailed to the Admiralty Islands, part of New Guinea. Margaret and Reo would be staying in the village of Peri ("PER-ry"), on the island of Manus ("MAH-noose").

The people of Peri lived in houses on stilts above the waters of a lagoon. They were fishermen and traders, exchanging dogs' teeth, shell money, and beads among themselves and with the people of the other islands for food and goods.

Names were very private on Manus, and the villagers of Peri were horrified when Reo called his wife by her real name. Instead, they named Reo "Moeyap" (MOY-yap)—Western Man—and Margaret "Piyap" (PEE-yap)—Woman of the West. They were delighted when Margaret had learned enough of their language to take notes about their trades. "Now we won't have to quarrel anymore," they said, "for the Piyap can write it all down."

Reo would be studying the villagers' religion. Margaret was interested in how children's thoughts changed as they became adults. She had brought with her 1,000 sheets of drawing paper—in the end, the children made more than 35,000 drawings—along with beads, balloons, toys, and rice and tobacco to trade to the adults for fish to eat.

The people of Peri had none of the easy hospitality of the Samoans. They were interested in their white visitors mostly because of what they had to trade. The children were delightful—open and intelligent. They played all day long, fishing, swimming, or boating until they were tired, resting, then playing again. They had no chores to perform. They were never corrected. Still, they grew up to be as secretive and competitive as their parents. Adult behavior is always the stronger, Margaret said.

Margaret broke her ankle and was very ill several times with malaria on Manus. Even so, it would be the best field trip she and Reo took together.

Their life got much more complicated when they returned to New York. Margaret's book on Samoa was a best seller. It was praised by anthropologists, journalists, and writers alike. Margaret was hurrying to finish her second book, about Peri, to be called *Growing*

Reo Fortune

Up in New Guinea. She was interviewed, and she was invited to make more speeches. One of her friends said, "*Coming of Age in Samoa* put anthropology on the map and caused youngsters to flock to it."

It was hard for Reo to accept Margaret's astonishing success. He had other complaints as well. The rural New Zealander felt imprisoned in a small city apartment. He and Margaret had very little money to spend. He had nothing in common with Margaret's friends. He was much happier in the field.

At the end of 1931, they returned to New Guinea, this time to the main island. There they would study three very different peoples: the mild Mountain Arapesh ("AIR-ah-pesh"); the Mundugumor ("Mun-DOO-geh-more"), a fierce tribe living on the bank of the Yuat ("YOO-ot") River; and the Tchambuli ("Cham-BOO-lee").

Margaret was interested in the differences in behavior between men and women. Among the Arapesh, she found, there were no differences at all. Both parents expected to take care of the children. Both men and women were gentle and sensitive to the needs of others. Doing anything to make another person angry was frowned upon. The Arapesh were kind, but they weren't very interesting.

The Mundugumor were the exact opposites of the Arapesh. They had been cannibals until four years before. Both men and women were expected to be ferocious. If the Mundugumor were angry—which was often—they scratched and bit and had temper tantrums. Men wanted girl children; women wanted boy children. Sometimes babies were thrown into the river to drown by one or the other parent because they were the wrong sex.

Margaret complained that there were far too many white people traveling up and down the Yuat. She and Reo were also disappointed that the Mundugumor had postponed all quarrels for the length of their stay.

Anthropologists learn a great deal from seeing who quarrels with whom about what.

Margaret and Reo were beginning to get on each other's nerves. They argued about their work. Reo was very unsympathetic when Margaret had several serious attacks of malaria. She thought the Mundugumor brought out the worst in him. She realized, she said, that she was "living with a crank." In a letter to a friend, Reo said much the same thing about Margaret.

Reo and Margaret moved again, to study the people who lived on Tchambuli Lake. The lake was lovely, its dark surface dotted with white, pink, and blue flowers. However, Reo and Margaret had to learn their third language in less than a year.

As Margaret wrote to Ruth Benedict, "The dashed language is really awful. Learning five-syllable words and six-syllable names is very wearing. . . . A dark rainy morning . . . a very horrible sore to [treat, for one of the villagers]—half a toe eaten away and a horrible stench . . . horrible lot of gnats."

Margaret soon discovered there were strong differences between the sexes at Tchambuli. The women managed the business affairs and ran the household. The men loafed, carving, painting, styling their hair, and gossiping.

While they were living on Lake Tchambuli, Margaret and Reo teamed up with a young British anthropologist named Gregory Bateson. Six foot five, thin, messy, Gregory looked like an overgrown teenager. He was sensitive and intelligent. In New Guinea off and on since 1928, Gregory was also very lonely. He had written his mother, "I feel I could scarcely face another anthropological expedition without a partner."

Margaret, Gregory, and Reo worked closely together, comparing notes on the peoples they had studied—and Margaret and Gregory fell in love.

Margaret and Greg

In the spring of 1933, the three of them left New Guinea. Margaret would not see Reo again until long after they divorced. She and Gregory Bateson would be married within three years.

six

A HOUSEHOLD WORD

Mead was becoming a household word. "Woman explorer," the newspapers called her. "They Kill Babies," began an article about the Mundugumor. Margaret welcomed the attention. To her way of thinking, the larger the audience the better. She was in New York City, working on another book, writing articles, making speeches. Wasn't the whole point to get people interested in the rest of the world, to show Americans other ways of seeing and doing things?

Margaret traveled to Ireland, where she met Gregory. He came to the United States, to give lectures at Columbia University and the University of Chicago. They began to plan a field trip together. For Margaret, it would be the perfect partnership. She and Gregory had the same interests, the same goals, and similar personalities. There was no feeling of competition between them.

They were married in Singapore in 1936. Then they headed for the island of Bali, in Indonesia. Bali was an anthropologist's dream. It was a beautiful green island where more than a million people spoke the same language. Margaret and Gregory were able to hire a Balinese secretary who knew English. There was an English-speaking community of artists, musicians, and dancers on the island, from the United States and Europe. The food was delicious. The Batesons—Margaret didn't seem to mind being called by Gregory's name—lived in a small, modern house they had had built.

Of the Arapesh, Gregory had said, "They cannot tell you anything, and don't do anything, and nothing happens all the time." On Bali, there was always something going on. There were so many people, and so many villages, and temples, and dancers, that the Batesons could see twenty birth feasts instead of just one, or sixty versions of the same dance, or one hundred festivals.

Gregory and Margaret took 25,000 still photographs and thousands of feet of movie film. One of the movies they produced, *Trance and Dance in Bali*, is still used to show what anthropologists can do with film. The Batesons' work was interrupted by the world outside, however. World War II was beginning. They left Bali for New York in 1939. Margaret was thirty-seven years old, and she was expecting a baby.

Margaret was thrilled. As a child, she had loved taking care of younger children. She never liked pets, because children were so

Gregory and Margaret

Trance dancers

much more interesting. Both her mother and her grandmother had had children *and* careers. Margaret had always assumed she would do the same.

Now she was busy making plans for the baby. She would breast-feed, although it would be twenty years or more before breast-feeding became popular in the United States. Margaret also had plans for the birth itself. She wanted to deliver the baby in a squatting position. That was the usual way among the peoples Margaret had studied.

In that, Margaret was forty years ahead of her time. Her baby was born in New York City on December 8, 1939. Margaret had given up on the squatting delivery, but had insisted on as little anesthesia as possible, a photographer to film the birth, and a pediatrician to be present, the young Dr. Benjamin Spock. The delivery-room nurses had all been shown a Bateson-Mead film, *First Days in the Life of a New Guinea Baby*.

Everything went well. At the end, Margaret was given medication to slow things down a little—the photographer had to run out to her car for another flashbulb.

Gregory Bateson was in England, trying to decide how to put his skills to best use in the war effort. He and Margaret had already decided on a name for the baby. "Mary" was for one of Gregory's aunts; "Catherine" was for Margaret's little sister Katherine. Mary Catherine Bateson would be called Cathy by her parents.

First Margaret took Cathy home to the Meads' house in Philadelphia. There Margaret began to draw on all the things she had learned on her field trips about rearing children.

After six weeks, Gregory returned. The Bateson family moved back to New York, renting an apartment from an old friend of Margaret's, Lawrence Frank. Larry Frank was a social scientist, too. He had a big house in Greenwich Village and five—soon to be six—children. The Franks were to be a second family for Cathy Bateson as she grew up.

An English nanny was found for the baby, and Margaret went back to work, arranging her appointments around Cathy's feeding schedule. She worked part-time at the museum and taught a class at New York University. She and Gregory were putting together a book with their photographs of Bali.

At the same time, Margaret was working on a book about Americans in wartime. "When will and when won't an American fight?" she asked in *And Keep Your Powder Dry.* "Where lies the American strength and the American weakness?" And "Why is it so important for us to think we're right?"

Americans, she wrote, have a strong sense of "fair play." They don't like fighting someone weaker than themselves. They fight best when the other person starts it. And they must believe their cause is just, that it will lead to a "new and better world." Margaret was doing fieldwork in her own country, using anthropology to help win the war.

She had almost finished a second book about Americans when the atomic bomb was dropped on Hiroshima in 1945. "At that point I tore up every page," she said. "Every sentence was out of date. We had entered a new age."

Humankind had the power to destroy itself. Now the important thing was to unite the peoples of the world, not to divide them. Anthropologists must use their knowledge "to help human beings live, without war, on one planet."

Gregory Bateson had spent the last part of the war in India and Burma, as a member of the British Office of Strategic Services. He returned to New York in 1946, after he and Margaret had been apart for three years. They were no longer working in the same direction. Gregory was most interested in ideas. Margaret wanted to put ideas into action.

She and her husband worked at different

speeds as well. Gregory said of Margaret, "She could sit down and write three thousand words by eleven o'clock in the morning, and spend the rest of the day at the museum." She was pure energy, he said, and he just couldn't keep up.

When Margaret tried to pull Gregory along with her, he pulled away . . . far away, first across town and then all the way to California.

seven

IDEAS "LYING AROUND LIKE PENCILS"

Margaret Mead, Margaret Mead,
Helps to fill our country's need
Thinks our culture is much lower
Than the one that's in Samoa. . . .

went a verse after the war. Margaret's every word made news. She lectured at Vassar College and Stanford University, at the University of California and at Harvard. "We must hurry, hurry, hurry to get the records in before the last primitive man puts on clothes and starts paying taxes," she told her audiences. Otherwise, "we shall have lost priceless information about what we might have been like *ourselves*."

Once she was asked if it upset her to see the primitive peoples she had studied changing, adopting the modern way of life. No, Margaret was quick to answer. "When a people's way of living is out of step with the larger world," she said, "they cannot take a dignified place in that world."

No one was more in step with the larger world than Margaret. She was more interested in children than in adults, more interested in women than in men, but she spoke on every phase of human life: marriage, religion, hunger, even Santa Claus—he was fine as an "expression of gift-giving," she said. But children should not be told Santa is a real person—it is too disappointing to them when they discover he isn't.

Margaret left ideas "lying around like pencils." She wanted them to be picked up and used, the quicker the better. Her friend Larry Frank once told her, "We might have a field day figuring out why you get people mad, or why they get mad at you." She provoked arguments, Margaret answered, to get people to think.

Now it was not just vanishing societies that had to be saved. The whole world needed a giant rescue operation. Margaret, with her talks and articles, classes, radio shows, and television appearances, brought more young people into anthropology than anyone else ever had. She had a vast network of friends with whom she kept in touch by telephone, letters, and memos—while she herself was off to a new meeting in a new city.

Margaret made at least one important new friend every couple of months, she said, and she kept them all. She might not see someone for years, but that person was still in Margaret's mind. She would pick up their conversation just where they'd left off.

"Friendship means freedom of choice," Margaret declared. "A friend chooses, and is chosen." Friends shared their ideas and feelings with her, and took care of her daughter while she was traveling. Friends were to become even more important. The marriage Margaret had most wanted to last had ended. She and Gregory Bateson were divorced in 1950. Margaret would never really get over it.

Margaret had not given up fieldwork. In a book for young readers, Margaret Mead wrote: "The mere suggestion of a field trip sets an anthropologist to sniffing the air." In 1953, she returned to the island of Manus, where she and Reo Fortune had done fieldwork in 1928. Margaret collected more drawings from the children of Peri village and took hundreds of rolls of film.

Gone were the dogs' teeth and shell money. Even the skulls of the villagers' ancestors, always displayed inside their houses, had disappeared. The American forces had been stationed on Manus during World War II, and things had changed. The people still loved to trade, however. In Peri, they spent all day making and returning loans of cigarettes.

The villagers remembered Margaret's first visit in great detail: who had paddled a canoe for Piyap, what she'd called the little boys who cooked for her, how Piyap and Moeyap had worked eighteen hours at a time. It was almost like a family gathering, Margaret said. She ordered a huge cargo of gifts for them from Australia.

As she was preparing to sail away, a villager told her, "Now, like an old sea turtle, you are going out to sea to die, and we will never see you again." He was wrong. Margaret would return to Manus with television crews, and also to Bali.

In 1960, Margaret broke her ankle, the same ankle she had fractured on Manus on her first visit. It healed in a cast, but it would always be weak. Instead of using a cane, Margaret chose a long forked stick, made of cherry wood and as high as her shoulder. She had gained weight and taken to wearing flowing capes. In a cape, carrying her forked stick, Margaret looked almost magical—like an Old Testament prophet, she said, or a kindly witch.

The thing Margaret was most afraid of in the world, she had told a friend, was being bored. There was little likelihood of that. Being Margaret Mead meant "having to decide between too many things I ought to be doing." She never stopped for a moment. Some people felt that the rushing here and there helped her to avoid the feeling of loneliness she never discussed. Margaret still carried a photograph of Gregory Bateson with her when she traveled.

Mary Catherine Bateson was now an anthropologist herself. She had married John Barkev Kassarjian. He was a Harvard-educated engineer, born in Syria of Armenian parents. In 1969, Mary Catherine gave birth to Sevanne Margaret. Margaret Mead was a grandmother, with a new way to feel, and a new child to

Peré 1975

Mask making

study. "I suddenly realized that through no act of my own," Margaret said, "I had become a biological relative to a new human being." It was one of the most exciting things that had happened to her.

In 1976, the year of the United States Bicentennial, Margaret Mead turned seventy-five. The American Association of Anthropologists held an all-day celebration for her in Boston, with speeches by friends and fellow scientists. Gregory Bateson joined her for the occasion.

In December of that year, the American Museum of Natural History and Margaret's publisher took out a full-page advertisement in *The New York Times*: HAPPY BIRTHDAY, MARGARET MEAD. The museum also gave her a five-day party of speeches, films, and exhibits. "I've been treated with extraordinary love and an enormous amount of undeserved praise, and I ought to be embarrassed, and I'm not," Margaret joked.

She had once said she would like to die on

her knees in church, but it wasn't to be. Margaret died in a hospital bed of cancer of the pancreas on November 15, 1978.

The news of her death was broadcast around the world and heard by former students and friends as far away as Sumatra, Nigeria, and the village of Peri in New Guinea. At a memorial service held at the museum, Gregory Bateson said, "Margaret Mead was hard, if not impossible, to pigeonhole." She had produced thirty-nine books; more than a thousand articles; many tapes, records, and films. She had won forty awards.

Margaret Mead was one of the great thinkers of our time. She spent her life learning more, seizing ideas from everything she heard or read, from everybody she met, and putting them to good use.

She was buried next to the little Episcopal church in Buckingham where she was baptized as a girl. On her tombstone is written: "To cherish the life of the world."

When Margaret Mead was a child, she was pleased to discover that her sign of the zodiac was Sagittarius, the Archer. It made her feel that she could "run as far as anyone, and shoot a little farther." And run she did, from one country to another, from one meeting to the next, springing from idea to idea with her arrows at the ready. Her target was enormous—all of humankind.

As an anthropologist, Margaret said, it was her job not only to learn all she could about other societies, but to share what she had learned. I feel that she is still sharing her knowledge, through the books, articles, movies, and interviews she left to the world. The American Museum of Natural History in New York City screens her movies each year during the Margaret Mead Film Festival. And there is a wealth of printed material about her, some written by her, some by people who knew her well. The libraries at Columbia University have much of her work on their shelves. It was there that I began to learn about Margaret Mead, when I was a student at Barnard College.

Margaret spent her life looking, listening, and asking questions. She felt strongly that not only could she make a difference in the world—you can, too.

S.S.

TIMELINE / INDEX

Meet More
WOMEN OF OUR TIME

RACHEL CARSON
SCIENTIST, AUTHOR, ENVIRONMENTALIST

Rachel Carson was always fascinated by the ocean. As a child, she dreamed of it and longed to see it. As a young woman, she felt torn between her love for nature and her desire to pursue a writing career. Then she found a way to combine both. Rachel had a talent for writing and talking about science in a way that everyone could understand and enjoy. With her controversial book, *Silent Spring*, Rachel Carson changed the way we look at our planet.

AMELIA EARHART
PIONEER, VOYAGER, PILOT

A pioneer in aviation, Amelia Earhart was the first woman in the world to fly across the Atlantic Ocean, and the first person to cross it twice. Her piloting career was built on passion, determination, and hard work, and led to broken records, many news headlines, and correspondence with the U.S. president. Her life became a great adventure story—and a great mystery, too. In 1937, on an around-the-world flight, Amelia disappeared. Today, her courage and sprit remain an inspiration to everyone who flies or dreams of adventure.

LAURA INGALLS WILDER
SCHOOLTEACHER, JOURNALIST, WRITER

Laura Ingalls Wilder grew up during the pioneer days of America. To the delight of millions of readers, she recounted her girlhood memories in the Little House series, including *Little House on the Prairie*. This is the true story of her life, and how she came to be known as one of the most important children's book authors of all time.

BABE DIDRIKSON
ATHLETE, OLYMPIAN, CHAMPION

She loved to boast that she would be one of the world's greatest athletes—and soon no one could deny it. As a teenager, Babe Didrikson became a star basketball player. Later, she won two Olympic gold medals for track and field, and then went on to an unparalleled career as a golfer. Strong and determined, Babe always played like a true champion.

HELEN KELLER
AUTHOR, SCHOLAR, ADVOCATE

"Forget that I am deaf and blind and think of me as an ordinary woman," wrote Helen Keller—but she was anything but ordinary. When Helen was growing up, there were almost no facilities to help handicapped students. Still, she learned to speak, read, and write. It wasn't enough to prove that she could do anything. Helen wanted other handicapped people to know that they could, too. And Helen achieved her purpose: The world saw her not only as a woman, but an extraordinary human being.